# For A New Harmony Millennium

## AN INTRODUCTION TO METATONAL MUSIC

## Randy Sandke

EXCLUSIVELY DISTRIBUTED BY

HAL•LEONARD®
CORPORATION

7777 W. BLUEMOUND RD. P.O. BOX 13819 MILWAUKEE, WI 53213

SECOND FLOOR MUSIC

Cover design and book design: Terry Chamberlain
Music engraving: Osho Endo
*Brownstones* solo transcription : Don Sickler
Photograph of Mr. Sandke: Ron Schwerin
A Don Sickler Production

# Harmony For A New Millennium

## AN INTRODUCTION TO METATONAL MUSIC

### Randy Sandke

# Introduction

**H**armony is the crowning achievement of western music. It is also the underpinning of the tonal system. Since the renaissance, composers and theorists have been obsessed with analyzing and utilizing vertical combinations of tones. Harmonic relationships have also provided the basis for form in tonal music, all the way from the 12-bar blues to the symphony.

In the 20th century, however, a desire to break the bounds of tonality has cast harmony into a lesser role. The western classical tradition has sought to replace harmony (which is derived from the natural properties of acoustics) with such intellectual constructs as serialism (Schoenberg), probability (Xenakis), and even chance (Cage). In the jazz of our own time there is a division between the schools of harmonic and "free" improvising.

Yet in both the jazz and classical fields, a large area of harmony has been overlooked and never systematically explored. This is the realm of metatonal music ("meta" being the Greek word for "beyond"). In *Part One* I will identify and organize all four-note chords which lie beyond the tonal system and which cannot be represented by conventional chord symbols. To these I assign new symbols.

*Part Two* deals with deriving melodic material from these metatonal chords. I originally conceived of using this method in a jazz context, but it works equally well when applied to contemporary classical composition. The technique I recommend is to divide the octave into three four-note metatonal chords (one the fundamental sonority and the other two "complementary" chords) and use these as the source for melodic invention.

In *Part Three* I show how I have used these ideas in recorded examples of my own music. These examples include pieces for symphony orchestra as well as jazz quintet.

# Harmony
# For A New Millennium

## AN INTRODUCTION TO METATONAL MUSIC

## Randy Sandke

The art of jazz improvisation has taken many forms and spawned many styles in its brief history, ranging from the melodic players of the 1920s, through the harmonic improvisers of the 1940s, to the free players of the 1960s. For the last forty years or so a polarization has existed between practitioners of these last two styles—those musicians who use harmony as a basis for form and melodic improvisation, and those who ignore it, concentrating instead on melodic development, sound, texture, and sheer emotional intensity.

On the one hand, free players tend to feel that harmonic improvisation is too restrictive and outmoded, while harmonic players often feel that free jazz is tantamount to musical anarchy and incoherence. This dichotomy has become so familiar that we take it for granted, like some immutable law of nature. Although many musicians over the last few decades have attempted to straddle both styles, they are still essentially choosing between tonal harmony and no harmony at all.

Yet between these two extremes lies an area of music which has largely been overlooked and never systematically explored. What I propose here is a new style in which scales and tonality are dispensed with, yet harmony still serves as a basis for form and melodic improvisation. I call this metatonal music.

As its name implies, metatonal music deals with those chords that lie beyond the scope of traditional harmony, even as the harmonic vocabulary has been extended and elaborated in contemporary jazz. Metatonal chords tend to be more dissonant, unstable, and "anti-diatonic" than those in current use. For example, a reasonably well trained jazz musician would have no trouble playing on a C7, or even a Dmaj7♯5/A♭, or indeed over no chords whatsoever. But how would that same player relate to these harmonies?

Until now, intuition would have been the only guide. Metatonal music provides a sound and logical basis for approaching these new sonorities. Indeed it enables one to improvise freely yet coherently over any vertical combination of tones.

In *Part One*, the Index of Metatonal Chords, we shall identify, label, and catalogue these non-tonal harmonies. In *Part Two*, An Introduction to Metatonal Improvisation, we will see how these chords can provide a basis for melodic improvisation which departs from the standard tonal method of deriving scales from chords.

Another aim of metatonal music is to address the problem of form in contemporary music. For years tonal harmony provided the underlying structure or subtext for jazz improvisation. Although many musicians have chosen to avoid the familiar AABA patterns, twelve-bar blues and the like, nothing concrete has taken the place of the repeating chord cycle which generates both melodic material and structural cohesion. For whether a player chooses to play chromatically over ambiguous tonalities, or whether the player seeks to use his or her instrument for sonic effects, the common danger is that all solos begin to sound alike. These solos often bear little relation to the compositions in which they appear and are seemingly interchangeable from tune to tune. They are a far cry from the cohesive statements of Louis Armstrong and Charlie Parker, in which every note grows organically from its context and each solo bears a unique stamp of identity. Metatonal music seeks to solve this problem by again restoring harmony as the matrix for form and improvisation, yet by utilizing new harmonies in a new way.

Many critics and listeners will say that atonality is nothing new in jazz and will point to such important stylists as John Coltrane, Wayne Shorter, Ornette Coleman, or Cecil Taylor. I will consider each in turn to see how well the "atonal" label applies to their music.

First I must make a distinction between the terms "atonal" and "metatonal." Atonality describes music that has no apparent key center, whereas the spectrum encompassed by metatonal music contains any harmonic possibility ranging from the borderline of tonality through and including atonality. Furthermore, atonality, as conceived by Schoenberg, is linearly-based in that all melodic and harmonic material proceed from a twelve-tone row. Metatonal music, on the other hand, is harmonically-based: all melodic material is derived from an underlying harmony, as is the case with most tonal music.

Now let's examine the extent to which tonality, metatonality, or atonality have already been developed within the jazz context.

Coltrane may be seen as the first and perhaps greatest straddler of the sonic/harmonic split. His unique and most widely imitated contribution to the language of jazz is his technique of constant and rapid melodic modulation over an underlying modal harmony. Musicians refer to this kind of improvising as "playing outside the changes." But is it atonal?

I see it more as an extended appoggiatura where a whole phrase takes the place of one non-chord tone. The tonal laws of tension and resolution are stretched and delayed but in the end observed. It may be said that Coltrane achieved for jazz what Wagner accomplished for European classical music by pushing tonality to its limits. But his is essentially a tonal, albeit polytonal style.

The analogy of Debussy might serve to describe Wayne Shorter's coloristic approach to harmony. Familiar though ambiguous chords are released from their tonal moorings and left to float freely on their own course. Parallelism replaces functionality and a kind of tonal mist results. Nevertheless, the way Wayne Shorter improvises on his own compositions, while making the most of their inherent ambiguities, is still rooted in the tonal, scale-based method of improvisation. (Obviously I am not suggesting that Wayne Shorter's music sounds like Debussy's, any more than Coltrane sounds like Wagner, but rather that they share a similar relation to tonality.)

Ornette Coleman is a musician who made his reputation by abandoning harmony as an organizing principle. His "harmolodic" concept is an attempt to achieve an equality of musical elements so that no one facet will predominate. As he himself said in an article in *Downbeat* from July, 1983 (*Prime Time for Harmolodics*): "Harmony, melody, speed, rhythm, time, and phrasing all have equal position in the results."

In practice his playing is most often a mixture of pan-diatonicism (if not pure diatonicism) and expressive instrumental effects for which he has been credited as the progenitor of the "sonic" school. At times he does drift past the bounds of tonality, but usually in the pursuit of some melodic phrase that follows its own internal logic rather than any external scheme of note relations. So although his music touches on atonality this is a by-product of other musical interests and not a main concern.

Cecil Taylor is famous for running dense tone-clusters up and down the keyboard that surely defy anyone's notion of tonality. And yet when he slows down he can sound surprisingly tonal, almost Lisztian. A frequent use of octaves in the left hand reinforces this impression.

As with Ornette Coleman, the thread of logic in Cecil Taylor's music has more to do with the development of melodic motifs and changes in mood and energy levels than with the application of a specific method for relating vertical and horizontal sonorities. As A.B. Spellman has aptly stated in his portrait of Cecil Taylor in *Black Music, Four Lives*, "Cecil views the emphasis on tonality or lack of it as quite beside the point in his music."

So the concept of using harmony divorced from tonality as a governing principle for jazz improvisation is indeed something new and unexplored. An examination of the specifics of this approach will shed light on what has previously been an obscure terrain.

# I. Index Of Metatonal Chords

**T**his section outlines a system for organizing and labeling those chords that do not fit readily within the realm of tonality. This system is based on the idea that all such "unstable" chords contain at least one interval of a half-step. Certain diatonic chords also contain a half-step interval, but my thesis is that all borderline tonal and atonal chords (which I call metatonal chords) fall into this category. My purpose is to provide a framework for identifying and ordering these chords.

Some theorists might argue that whole-tone and quartal chords (which contain no half-step intervals) are atonal. Although these chords can have ambiguous functions I don't include them because they have been well-integrated into the tonal system over the last century and are generally less dissonant than the chords I am concerned with. Besides, whole-tone and quartal chords can already be designated with conventional chord symbols. For example: C7sus, Cm7(add4), C7♭5, C9+5♭5

Thus the half-step interval forms the basis of metatonal harmony, just as the interval of a third provides the basis of tonal harmony.

I have restricted myself to four-note chords because all the combinations from two to twelve notes may be seen as extensions of these chords, either by addition or subtraction. Furthermore, the four-note texture has been the standard in Western music for over five hundred years.

### A through G Series

The half-step interval is the starting place for all the chords we will examine. Our first chord beginning with this interval is a four-note cluster which for purposes of demonstration shall begin on middle C:

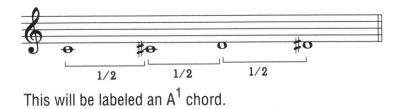

This will be labeled an A[1] chord.

By progressively raising the fourth (highest) note of this chord we arrive at the other chords of the "A" series:

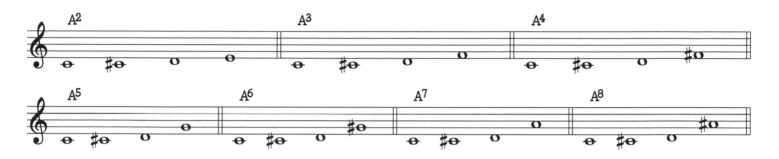

B natural is not included because this would result in a cluster starting on B, or a transposition of the A$^1$ chord:

In our example we began the chord on a C so it is designated a C$^{(A1)}$ chord. Transposed to a B it would be a B$^{(A1)}$ chord. (Perhaps it is appropriate that an A$^{(A1)}$ chord is made up of the notes B-A-C-H in their German spelling.) Needless to say, these chords may be inverted, voiced in any register, or transposed while still retaining their unique intervallic makeup and hence their designated chord symbol (as is true of their tonal counterparts.)

Following the "A" series, the next chord once again starts with our initial half-step interval:

1/2

However, this time we skip a whole-step before forming the next half-step interval. This results in the following chord:

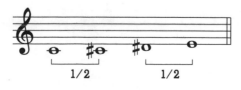

1/2          1/2

This shall be designated a B$^1$ chord. Again, since our example started on C, it is a C$^{(B1)}$ chord.

By progressively raising the fourth note we find the remaining chords of the "B" series:

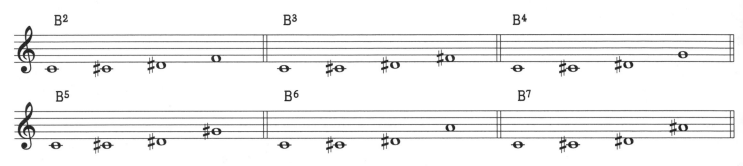

It will be noted that the B$^2$, B$^3$, B$^4$, B$^5$, and B$^7$ chords are composed of fragments of diatonic scales. For example:

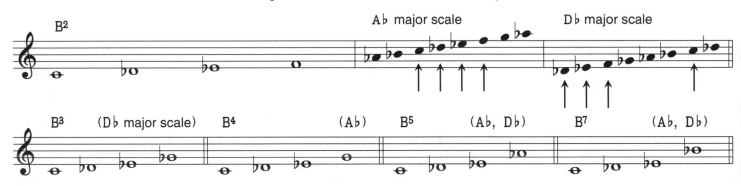

Once the labeling system has been fully explained I will sift through these chords and arrange them on a scale according to the dissonance of their intervallic structure. Diatonic chords will be separated from the other more ambiguous note combinations which are of course the main focus of this system.

We continue with the "C" series:

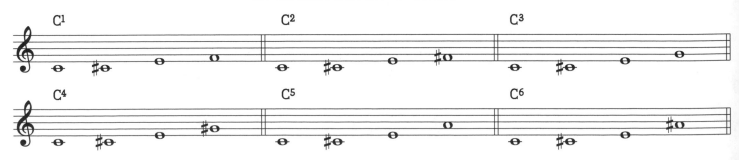

The "D" series:

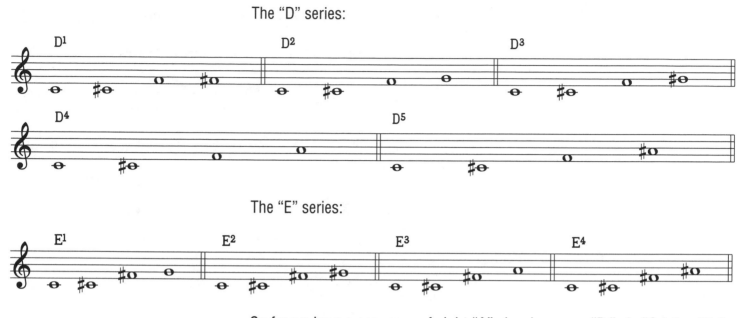

The "E" series:

So far we have a sequence of eight "A" chords, seven "B," six "C," five "D," and four "E" chords. However continuing our process of starting with a half-step interval and systematically raising the final two notes we find that the first chord of the "F" series:

has already been designated a G$^{(D1)}$:

However, the "F" series continues with two new chords:

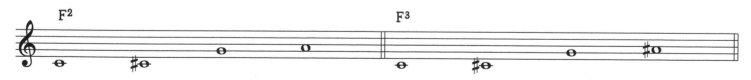

Similarly, the "G" series starts with:     or a G#$^{(C1)}$

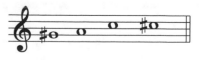

but continues with a new, though diatonic, chord:

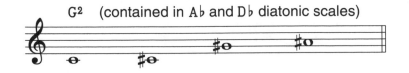

G² (contained in A♭ and D♭ diatonic scales)

Any further continuation of this system will result in a chord already designated.

For example, a hypothetical H¹: is already an A^(B1):

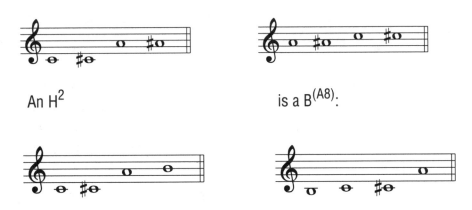

An H² is a B^(A8):

And so we end up with a total of 33 (or 8+7+6+5+4+2+1) four-note chords of different intervallic structure, each containing an interval of a half-step.

Here is the complete list:

These chords can be divided into three categories which I call "diatonic," "soft" and "hard." The diatonic chords are made up of pitches contained in diatonic scales. The "soft" chords contain only one half-step interval but are non-diatonic. This is a borderline category and many such chords may even have familiar tonal applications. However their ambiguity may be further enhanced in less tonal settings and they may be voiced in ways that would lean them more towards the atonal end of the spectrum. The following table will illustrate this point.

The "hard" chords contain at least two intervals of a half-step. They can conceivably have tonal usages as well, but their increased dissonance lends them to specifically atonal applications.

The purpose of this final categorization of chord types will become clear in the next section on metatonal improvisation. But also, since this system was designed to systematize non-tonal chords it is important to winnow these out from the more conventional chord types.

## DIATONIC CHORDS

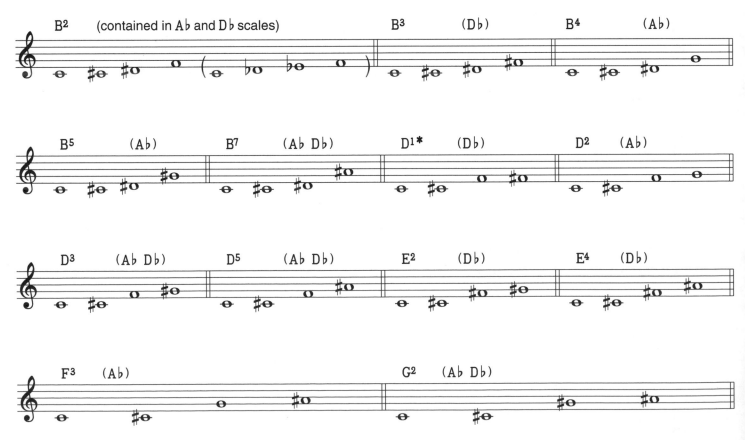

\* The D1 is the only chord listed in two categories. This is because it is a diatonic chord containing two half-step intervals.

## SOFT CHORDS

**HARD CHORDS**

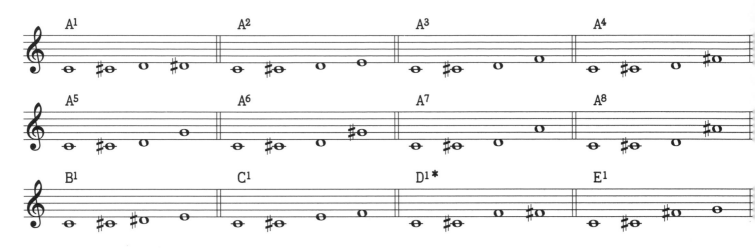

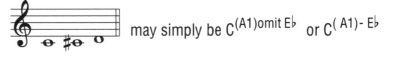

\* The D1 is the only chord listed in two categories. This is because it is a diatonic chord containing two half-step intervals.

As I said at the outset, we may also designate chords containing less or more than four notes. For instance:

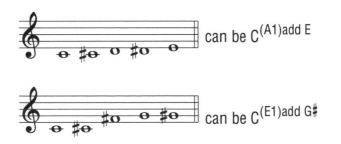

Similarly a five-note chord:

We may borrow the symbol ∪ (for union) from mathematical set theory and describe these same chords as a union of two four-note chords.

For example:

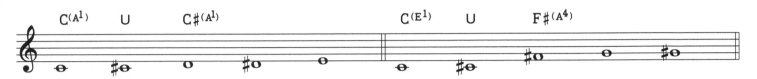

The practicality of using dual symbols becomes more apparent in chords of over five notes. For instance:

 could be $C^{(A1)} \cup D^{(C2)}$

The following chords illustrate this principle:

Seven-note chord:

Eight-note chord:

Nine-note chord:

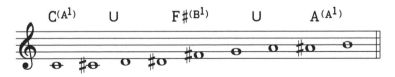

It may be noted that the same chord could be given an alternate though still accurate symbolic designation: $C^{(A1)} \cup D^{(C1)} \cup A^{(A1)}$. The important point is that an accurate designation can be given.

Ten-note chord:

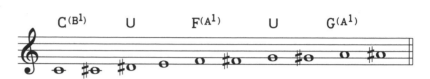

Eleven-note chords may be designated with multiple symbols or by simply writing ∨ the symbol (meaning the universal set) minus the one pitch not present: ∨-F

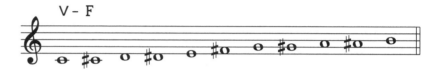

If one wishes to designate the chord containing all twelve tones, it can be written as a $C^{(A1)} \cup E^{(A1)} \cup G\sharp^{(A1)}$ chord. Of course the symbol "∨" alone would suffice.

Admittedly, dual and triple symbols are unwieldy and probably of little practical use. Writing the notes of the chord could be just as easy. However within the realm of four-note chords we have already found a wealth of new material to work with, and this will form the basis for the following section on metatonal composition and improvisation.

## II. An Introduction To Metatonal Improvisation And Composition

As we have just seen, my basic postulate for organizing and labeling non-tonal chords is that they contain at least one interval of a half-step. If this premise is accepted then all that follows is a closed logical system that proceeds with mathematical certainty.

Now we enter the more subjective realm of creating melodic material based on these chords. It is a situation where different possibilities present themselves and our task is to find the one that gives us the best results.

Therefore what I outline here is not the only approach one might use in working with metatonal chords, but it is the one that seems to me to be the most logical, organic, and easy to apply.

What are the criteria we are looking for? We want to have the freedom to use all twelve tones over any given chord so that our melodic lines are supple and malleable, and are free to go from one note to any other note. And yet we must have a structure to order these pitches in a way that relates them to our fundamental chord.

In tonal improvisation the chord provides a basis for note selection. The chord tones tones are linked with scale tones, and any other chromatic tone may be used in a decorative or coloristic way in the form of an alteration, extension, neighboring tone, etc. Here we have the requisite structure and yet the freedom to start anywhere and go anywhere as long as we observe the basic rule of tonality: non-chord tones must eventually resolve to chord tones; dissonance must resolve to consonance.

Of course the notion of a "non-chord" tone has changed over the years. Throughout its evolution the harmonic language of jazz has expanded to include as consonances many notes which were formerly considered dissonances. In the 1920s musicians improvised over simple triads and seventh chords much as rock musicians do to this day. And as in rock music, only the "blue notes" (flatted thirds and sevenths) managed to work their way into the vocabulary as unresolved dissonances. Musicologists view this phenomenon as an attempt to graft African vocalizations and modes onto western scales. In the 1930s sixths and ninths became common. With the advent of bebop, major sevenths, and raised ninths and thirteenths were accepted as fundamental chord tones (i.e., dissonances requiring no further resolution). As I mentioned earlier, the Coltrane and post-Coltrane school use cycles of chord progressions superimposed over an underlying harmony to create in effect a "non-chord" phrase.

In all these styles the player is free to use any chromatic pitch while still relating it in some way to the fundamental harmony. How are we to do this without the anchor of tonality?

The model of Schoenberg's tone-rows are of little help because no one, except perhaps a grand master of chess, can remember a sequence of twelve tones, much less spontaneously apply their transposition, inversion, retrograde, and retrograde inversion. Also, according to the twelve-tone system, a tone-row should function equally well over any vertical combination of tones derived from it. In practice this is not so, as the composer chooses from innumerable possibilities precisely how his harmony and melody should interact, relying on ear and intuition the way composers have for centuries.

So we must find a new model, based structurally on a given chord, one that allows the free use of all twelve tones but in a way specifically related to that fundamental chord. Further, we want to create a non-tonal texture to agree with the dissonance of these chords, one that can generate melodic lines that don't suggest patterns already associated with tonal improvisation.

I propose the following: we start with the four-note chord we are to improvise over:

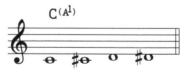

Next we divide the remaining eight notes of the chromatic scale into two other four-note chords. I call these "complementary" chords. It will be found that an octave can always be divided into three chords of the "hard" or "soft" type. For example:

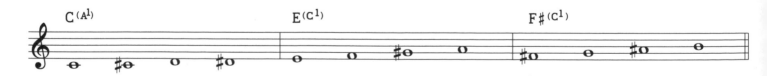

There are many ways to divide up the octave. Since we are interested in the non-tonal or more dissonant end of the tonal spectrum I favor the "hard" chords. Let's say we want to improvise on a $C^{(C1)}$ chord:

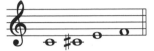

We can divide the octave into the following complementary chords:

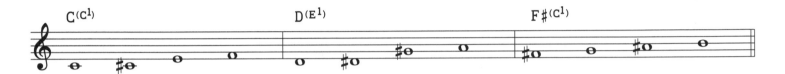

These three chords become pitch sets which provide us with our melodic material. The dissonant intervals from each group assure us of a consistently atonal melodic structure. The four-note groupings, once applied, are easy to remember. There are no rules as to their sequence, or how many notes from each group must be played. We may play none or all four. Notes from a single group may be played in any order, and one may jump from group to group in complete freedom—from any note in any group to any other note in any other group. In this way we may start on any note of the chromatic scale and jump to any other pitch while still retaining a basic relation to the underlying chord. For example:

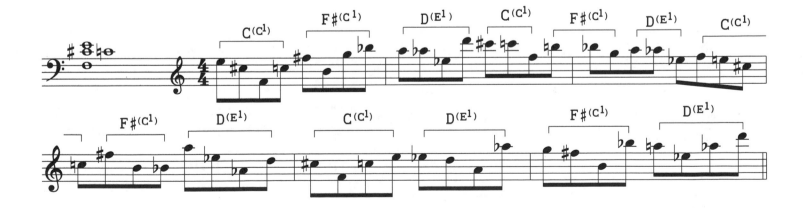

Of course we may start with our original chord and divide up the octave in different ways. For example:

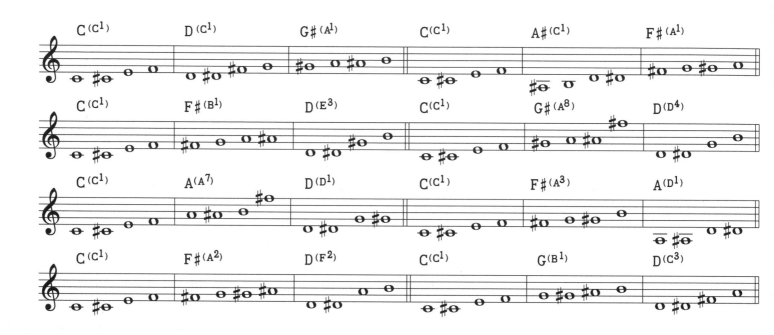

Here the improviser has a choice to discover those ways which work best.

Now we can sample some of the "hard" chords and see how to apply this principle of deriving complementary chords (for purposes of demonstration all of the initial chords begin on C, i.e., $C^{(A2)}$, $C^{(A3)}$, etc.):

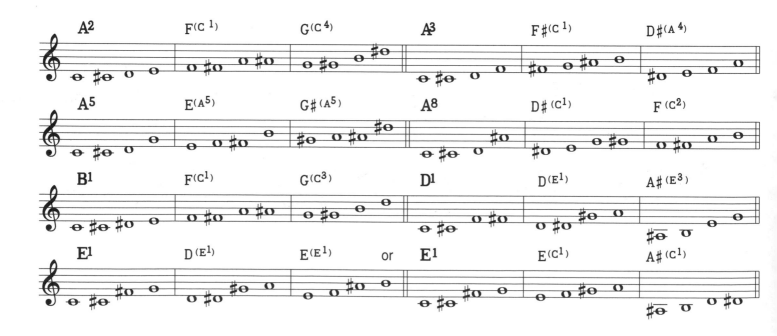

A short cut to finding complementary chords may be to use the $I^{(C1)}$, $II^{(D1)}$, $\flat V^{(C1)}$ formula as a basic model and make substitutions for other chords like this:

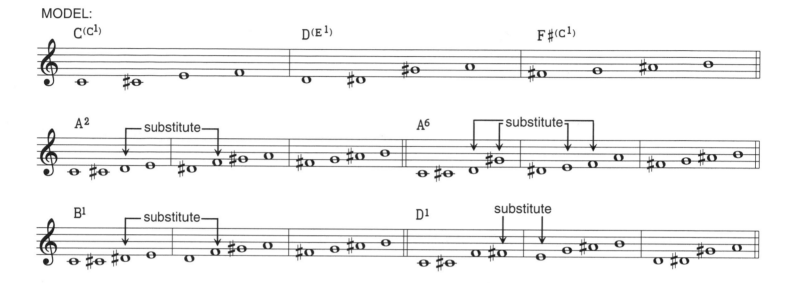

This system may even be used to play over tonal chords in a new way. As we found out in the last section, a D♭ major seventh is the same as a $C^{(D3)}$ chord. We can apply the same procedure of improvising using complementary chords over this familiar sonority:

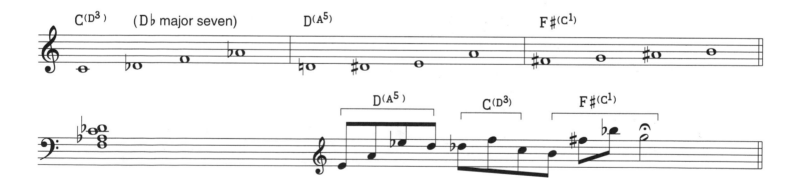

One may well wonder how difficult it is to master these melodic permutations to the point that one can improvise spontaneously with them. But I believe that this is no harder than learning to relate all the various scale possibilities to tonal chords in the traditional way.

We can expand our method to include chords containing more than four notes by extrapolating four-note chords from denser vertical combinations:

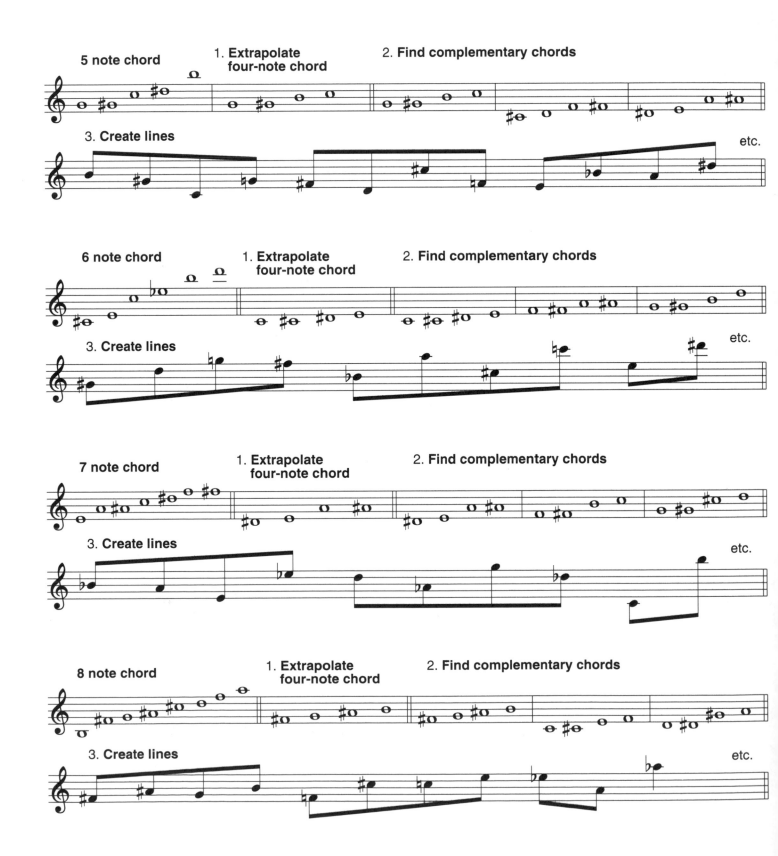

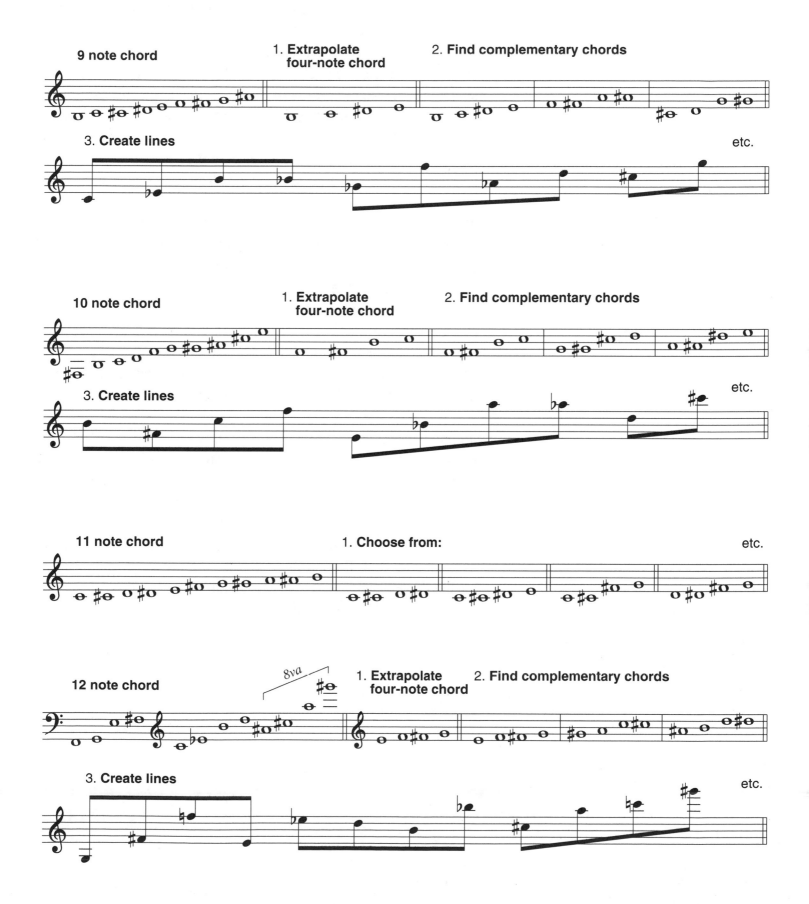

Of course the fundamental question is, do these mental gymnastics result in music that anyone wants to listen to? After all, the record of atonal music has not been a good one: very few works (some would say none) have entered the classical repertoire and the mere mention of the word is usually enough to send audiences to their feet in search of the nearest exit. However it is my belief that atonal melodies can be sensually appealing and beautiful. What I think most people object to in these pieces is an absence of recognizable form due to the absence of the building blocks of form: melody, motifs, chord progressions and identifiable phrases.

In their haste to form a new order to replace tonality composers have often gone to extremes and eliminated many aspects of music which are not strictly the province of "tonality." Dissonance has been liberated, all notes have been created equal, and yet the pursuit of happiness has eluded us. The backlash has already set in, in the form of minimalism and new-age music, neither of which, I would argue, represent the slightest advance in musical language or expression. Nevertheless, I believe that one can still be original without sacrificing sense and comprehensibility. And that one can be comprehensible without sacrificing subtlety.

It is certainly not my desire to add another useless theoretical treatise to the mounting (though in recent years mercifully diminishing) slag heap that has been accumulating over the last forty years. I am not interested in ideas that make sense on paper but result in the most bloodless and stultifyingly boring music that human beings can be forced to endure. Whether or not there is any validity to these ideas I have set forth here will only be revealed by the music itself. These ideas only have meaning as far as they can reverberate in sounds that have a meaning of their own, and one that requires no further explanation.

### GETTING STARTED: Two Metatonal Exercises

It is important to stress that one doesn't have to master all the harmonic and melodic possibilities outlined in the preceding chapters in order to work with metatonal music. I tend to concentrate on a few chords that I favor, such as those found in the following exercises. Remember that tonal music, from Bach to Charlie Parker, is derived from only a handful of chord types. A lot can be made out of a little.

I also suggest initially using a "modal" approach in working with metatonal chords: i.e., starting out with a long stretch of just one chord. In this way one can rapidly attain fluency in improvising metatonal lines.

**Exercise 1:** We will work with the following chord, a $C^{(C1)}$.

Any note of the chord may be considered the root:

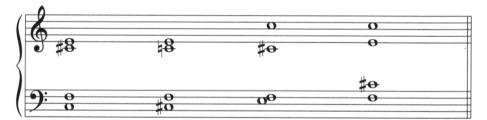

We can also voice the chord using only three notes:

Next we'll select two complementary chords:

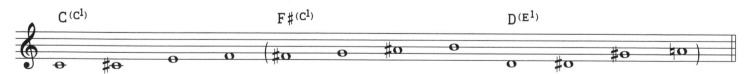

Now we are ready to create lines to play over our fundamental chord. (Note that the same melodic material can be used when either of the two complementary chords are considered the fundamental chord.)

Remember that you don't have to use all four notes of a chord before jumping to the notes of another. Also, you are free to jump from one chord to either of the other two.

The same melodic material can be used with chords of over 4 notes that contain the C$^{(C1)}$.

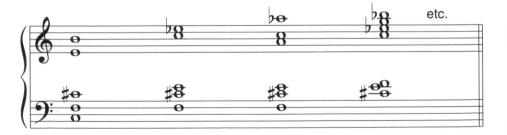

The C^(C1) chord shares three notes with a C♯ (D♭) major seventh chord. Likewise the F♯^(C1) (used as a complementary chord) bears the same relation to a Gmaj7. It is therefore possible to use the same metatonal lines in tonal situations that include these chords.

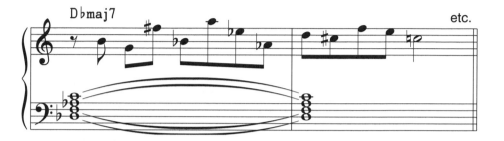

Find other tonal chords that share notes with the C^(C1).

**Exercise 2:** Now we'll take another chord, this time a C$^{(E1)}$:

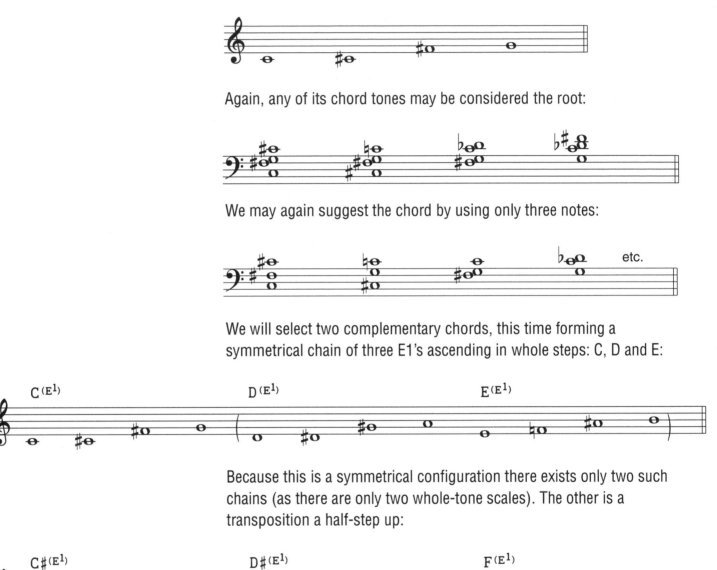

Again, any of its chord tones may be considered the root:

We may again suggest the chord by using only three notes:

We will select two complementary chords, this time forming a symmetrical chain of three E1's ascending in whole steps: C, D and E:

Because this is a symmetrical configuration there exists only two such chains (as there are only two whole-tone scales). The other is a transposition a half-step up:

Now we can create our melodic lines keeping in mind once again that we don't have to use every note from each chord, and that we are free to jump from the notes of one chord to those of any other:

Again, the same melodic material will work for chords of over five notes that contain the $C^{(E1)}$ (or $D^{(E1)}$ and $E^{(E1)}$ for that matter):

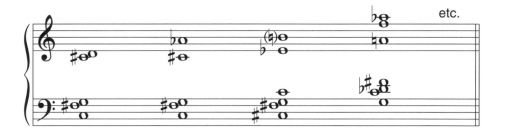

We can also use these lines over tonal chords as well, such as A7(#9) or E♭7(#9):

The same melodic material works equally well over sharp nine chords starting on B, F and C$\sharp$, G, because the complementary chords relate to these chords in the same way that the C$^{(E1)}$ relates to an A7$\sharp$9: i.e., they share three of the same notes (four in the case of an A13$\sharp$9).

# III. Metatonal Music In Real Time

As we've seen in the previous chapters, metatonal principles provide a map to harmonies which lie beyond the bounds of the tonal system. We are thus enabled to identify non-tonal chords, label them with chord symbols, and arrange them in hierarchy of increasing dissonance.

We've also seen how metatonal harmonies can be used to derive melodic material. This technique of dividing the octave into three "complementary" metatonal chords can be applied to both composition and improvisation. In this way it provides an alternative to serial technique in twelve-tone composition and can also fill in the harmonic gap between tonal jazz improvisation and "free" jazz.

What I want to do now is show how I've used these ideas in compositions of my own, in both jazz and classical contexts. These pieces are included, along with others that make use of metatonal principles, on my recording entitled *Awakening* on the Concord Concerto label (catalogue number CCD-42049-2) This album includes works for symphony orchestra, jazz quintet, and electronic instruments.

The first piece I'd like to discuss is also the first I wrote in the metatonal style for jazz quintet, and it is called ***Persistence***. The entire piece is derived from the following complementary chords:

**Example 1:**

In Example 2 we see the trumpet and tenor sax parts written on the top two staves with the piano part below. The first nine bars are a persistent (but varied) repetition of a single motif. Both it and the piano accompaniment are all taken from the $A\#^{(C1)}$ chord. At bar 10 the motif continues but introduces the $E^{(C1)}$ chord in both the melody and piano harmony. Note: all examples are written at concert pitch. Enharmonic spellings are sometimes used.

**Example 2:**

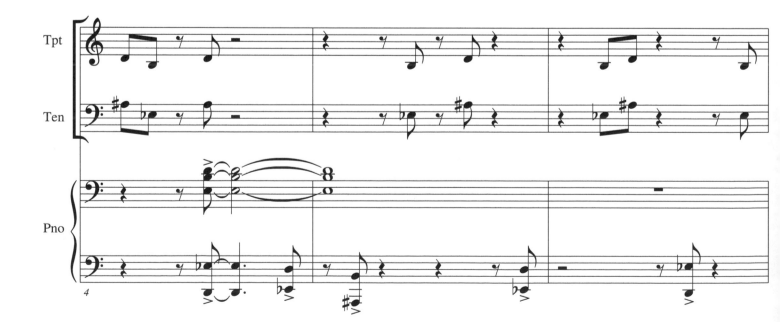

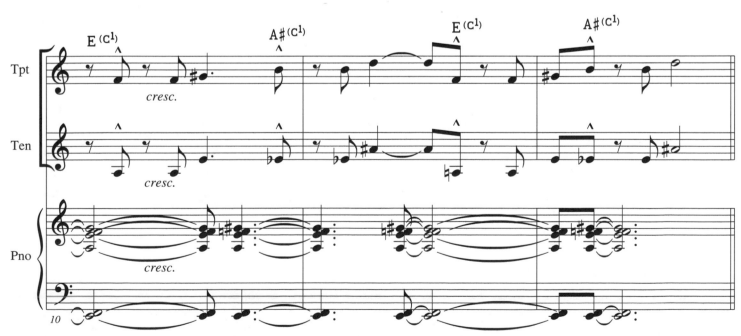

In Example 3, the last of the three complementary chords, a $C^{(E1)}$, is introduced, and the ensuing material makes free use of all three complementary chords. This piece is for the most part a straightforward text-book instance of metatonal writing. The only departure from the basic three complementary chords occurs in bars 48-49 where the horns play a figure that takes the $A\#^{(C1)}$ up in whole steps to the $E^{(C1)}$. Likewise in bars 53-54 the $C^{(E1)}$ chord is elaborated by an $E^1$ chord up a minor third. Note that as the piece progresses there becomes increasingly less congruence between the chords used in the melody and in the piano harmony (bars 60-63).

**Example 3:**

The improvised sections of **Persistence** (the piano and trumpet solos) are approached in the same way that the piece was composed: by making free use of the harmonies and melodies generated by the original three complementary chords. The three chords are written out for the bass, piano, and trumpet as they appear in Example 1. The bass player makes walking lines by circulating freely between these chords. Similarly, the piano derives the accompaniment from them, and the trumpet and piano their solos. This solo section is similar to modal improvisation in that one block of related harmonic and melodic material provides the basis for an entire ad-lib passage. The length of this passage in **Persistence** is left up to the discretion of the player.

Of course metatonal chords may change as frequently as in a bebop tune, but this requires much skill and practice on the part of the improviser (as it does in bebop), and care on the part of the composer to avoid creating a harmonic blur. Pieces I've recorded involving improvisation over more densely packed metatonal chords include **Awakening**, **Brownstones** (Stash ST-CD- 575), and **In a Metatone** (Concord CCD-4717). Even more extended use of metatonal chord progressions is made in such (soon to be released) compositions of mine as **The Mystic Trumpeter**, and **Symphony for Six**.

I've also used metatonal harmonies as a basis for composing pieces for orchestra. I consider **_Orphic Mystery_** to be a borderline tonal-atonal piece. For instance, the initial melody, played by solo trumpet, can be analyzed using conventional chord symbols:

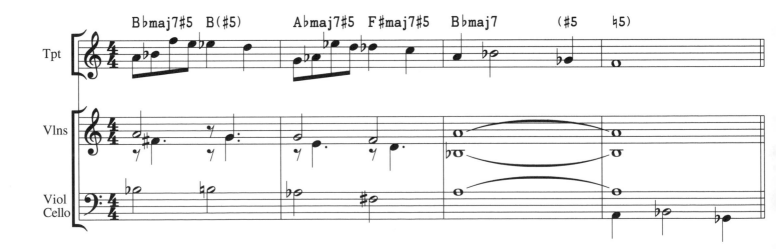

Or the harmony can be represented by metatonal symbols:

**Example 5:**

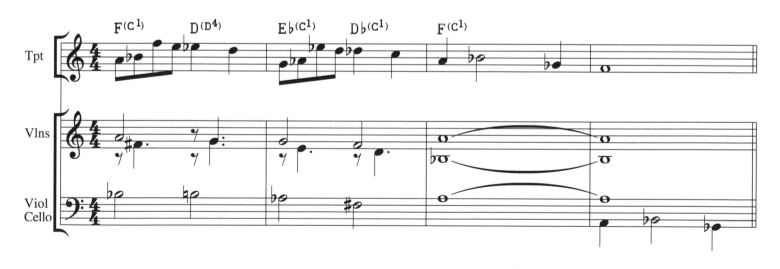

Further along in the piece, however, we run into harmonies that can only be labeled with metatonal symbols:

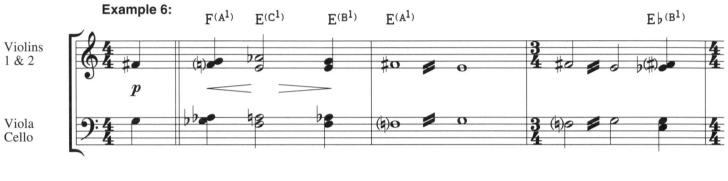

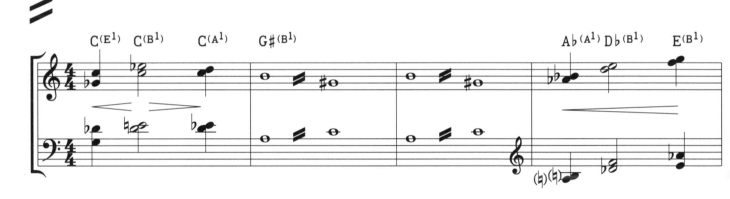

Example 8 shows a seemingly complex passage that is fact derived from the same configuration of the complementary chords we encountered in **_Persistence_**, albeit transposed down a half step. These three complementary chords are:

**Example 7:**

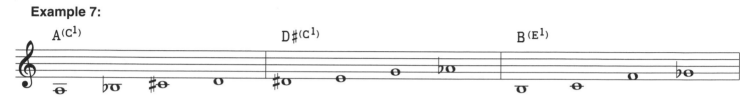

The strings alternate between all three chords in a running eighth-note figure. The trumpets reinforce the downbeats of this phrase while the horns take up the after beats. All of this occurs over a deceptively tonal open fifth played by basses, bassoons, and low brass, which is in fact derived from the $A^{(C1)}$ chord.

**Example 8:**

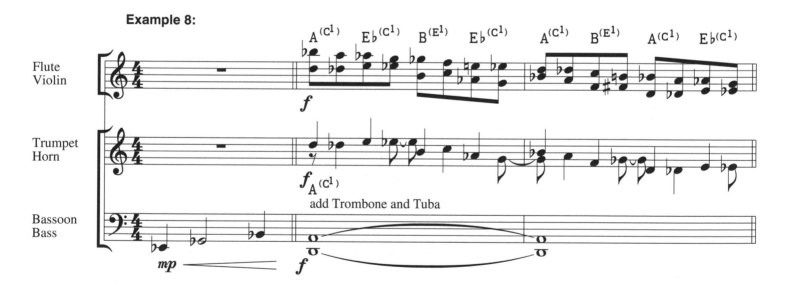

The final theme is a little more ambiguous because it is largely based on three-note harmonies. These may be suggested by the following chord symbols, although the fourth note only occasionally appears.

**Example 9:**

**Brownstones** is a duet for trumpet and piano which I recorded on my first album *New York Stories*, later released on CD as *The Sandke Brothers* (Stash ST-CD 575). Don Sickler has transcribed my solo note for note, and it contains many examples of improvised phrases derived from metatonal chords.

The form of the tune is basically AABA. Specifically the piece has an introduction followed by a statement of the theme (A repeated, B, and the A theme once again marked as letter C). A four-bar interlude follows at letter D. Letter E is an improvisation over the chords of the opening "A" theme for 16 bars. The "B" section returns at letter F. G and G1 mark the final statement of the "A" theme. The piano always plays the basic four-note metatonal chord indicated by the chord symbol. In the recording Jim McNeely sticks strictly to these notes but freely varies his rhythmic accompaniment.

My improvised passages adhere very closely to the metatonal principle of deriving all melodic material from the basic chord and its two complementary chords. Sometimes I begin my phrase with the fundamental chord as in bar 18. In that case I start with three notes of the $C^{(C1)}$, play three notes from the complementary $F\#^{(C1)}$, all four notes of the complementary $D^{(E1)}$, ending on three note from the $F\#^{(C1)}$.

In bar 32 the fundamental chord is a $C^{(A1)}$ which is a four-note cluster starting on C: C, C$\#$, D and D$\#$. While the piano sustains this harmony I play only on the complementary chords: in this case an $E^{(C1)}$ and an $F\#^{(C1)}$. Though my first note is an F from the $E^{(C1)}$, I go immediately to the $F\#^{(C1)}$ for nine notes, back to the $E^{(C1)}$ for four notes, and finally to the $F\#^{(C1)}$ for three notes. In measure 34 I move freely from the (complementary) $B^{(E1)}$ and $A^{(E1)}$ before finally resolving to the underlying $G^{(E1)}$. The main improvisation at letter E uses the fundamental $G(C1)$ with the complementary chords $C\#^{(C1)}$ and $A^{(E1)}$. Measures 39 and 45 are an $F\#^{(C1)}$, with $G\#^{(E1)}$ and $C^{(C1)}$ serving as complementary chords.

It is important to note that the fundamental harmony can appear anywhere within a phrase, or may not be stated at all (as in the case of measure 32): what is important is that all the melodic material ultimately derives from the basic chord and its two complements.

Randy Sandke

*As recorded by RANDY SANDKE on THE SANDKE BROTHERS (Stash ST-CD 575)*

# Brownstones

RANDY SANDKE

TRUMPET

I realize that the analysis of my improvisation on **Brownstones** may appear to some overly fussy and pedantic on paper. Many creative musicians value intuition over all else and may consider the ideas I've outlined here too restrictive (though as I've already pointed out, they're no more so than the laws governing tonal music). However, it's been my experience that the greater the discipline, the greater the freedom attained. The best improvisations sound composed, and the best compositions sound like brilliant improvisations. We should never lose sight of our main objective: to achieve unity in freedom while speaking in a new voice.

As I said at the end of the previous chapter, theories are useless unless they lead to useful results; in this case the creation of music that some people perceive as pleasing or stimulating. If these pieces I have written using metatonal ideas do generate interest I have been successful. Or, if these ideas are adopted by others who do the same, I have also achieved my purpose. Only time will tell. All I know is that these techniques have led me to the creation of works I wouldn't have been able to produce otherwise.

# Glossary

**Metatonal**: literally "beyond" tonal. A way of composing or improvising that involves the use of chords that lie beyond the scope of conventional tonal harmony. Also a method of deriving melodic material from the use of complementary chords.

**Hard Chord:** A vertical configuration of three notes or more that includes two or more intervals of a half-step.

**Soft Chord:** A vertical configuration of three notes or more that includes one interval of a half-step.

**Complementary Chords:** Three four-note chords that together form all twelve notes of the chromatic scale.

**Randy Sandke**

An exceptionally versatile trumpet player and composer, Randy Sandke has performed and recorded with a diverse array of musicians including Kenny Barron, Ray Brown, Michael Brecker, Benny Goodman, Dizzy Gillespie, Benny Carter, Frank Wess, Roswell Rudd, Wycliffe Gordon, Ray Anderson, Dick Hyman, Roland Hanna, Buck Clayton, Clark Terry, Flip Phillips, Marty Ehrlich, Louis Bellson, Ken Peplowski, Jon Hendricks, Joe Williams, John Pizzarelli, and George Wein's Newport All-Stars. Mr. Sandke has toured Europe numerous times, as well as Japan, Canada, India, and the U.S., performing at festivals, clubs and concerts throughout the world.

He has recorded several albums as a leader, and since 1993, Mr. Sandke has been a Concord Jazz and Nagel-Heyer recording artist. Mr. Sandke has appeared on television in Sweden, Switzerland, Germany, France and Japan, and in the U.S. in "Let's Dance," a PBS special with Benny Goodman. He has played on several movie soundtracks including "The Cotton Club," and five Woody Allen films.

Over fifty of Randy Sandke's compositions have been recorded, ranging from works for jazz quintet to big band to symphony orchestra. His pieces have been played in Carnegie Hall and Avery Fischer Hall at Lincoln Center. The Carnegie Hall Jazz Band has performed six of his suites, and Mr. Sandke is also the recipient of two NEA composition grants.

# Discography

Recorded pieces using metatonal techniques:

**Awakening; Fugue State 1 and 2; Orphic Mystery; Overture For The Year 2000; Persistence; Sea Change** (Randy Sandke, *Awakening*, Concord Concerto CCD-42049-2); also **Prelude to a Kiss** (Ellington, Sandke arrangement)

**Brownstones** (*The Sandke Brothers*, Stash ST-CD-575)

Introduction to Thelonious Monk's **Humph** (Randy Sandke, *Get Happy*, Concord Jazz CCD- 4598)

**In a Metatone** (Randy Sandke, *Calling All Cats*, Concord Jazz CCD-4717)

**Inside Out**, **Plumbing The Depths, Sforzando** (Randy Sandke, *Inside Out*, Nagel-Heyer Records); also **Creole Love Call** (Ellington, Sandke arrangement)

Extended pieces performed but currently unrecorded:

**The Mystic Trumpeter** (Performed in 1992 at Greenwich House, NYC)

**Genesis** (Performed in 1994 at Avery Fischer Hall at Lincoln Center, NYC)

**Symphony for Six** (Performed in 1995 at Merkin Concert Hall, NYC)

Parts of the following pieces commissioned for and premiered by the Carnegie Hall Jazz Band contain metatonal passages:
> **New Orleans Joys**
> **King Louis**
> **The Hill On The Delta**